MW01179029

DEHAL

Fact Finders™

Biographies

Roberto Clemente
Baseball Legend

by Nick Healy

Consultant:

Jim Gates
Library Director
National Baseball Hall of Fame and Museum
Cooperstown, New York

Capstone
press

Mankato, Minnesota

Fact Finders is published by Capstone Press,
151 Good Counsel Drive, P.O. Box 669, Mankato, Minnesota 56002.
www.capstonepress.com

Library of Congress Cataloging-in-Publication Data
Healy, Nick.
    Roberto Clemente : baseball legend / by Nick Healy.
    p. cm. — (Fact finders. Biographies. Great Hispanics)
    Includes bibliographical references and index.
    ISBN-13: 978-0-7368-5442-9 (hardcover)
    ISBN-10: 0-7368-5442-8 (hardcover)
    1. Clemente, Roberto, 1934–1972—Juvenile literature. 2. Baseball players—Puerto
Rico—Biography—Juvenile literature. I. Title. II. Series.
GV865.C3H43 2006
796.357'092—dc22   2005022584

Summary: An introduction to the life of Roberto Clemente, the baseball superstar from
    Puerto Rico who is remembered for his talent on the field and his humanitarian
    efforts off the field.

Editorial Credits
Megan Schoeneberger, editor; Juliette Peters, set designer; Linda Clavel and Scott Thoms,
    book designers; Wanda Winch, photo researcher/photo editor

Photo Credits
Corbis/Bettmann, 11, 17, 24
Duane Rieder, Official Clemente Family Archivist, 9, 13, 18–19, 26
Getty Images Inc./Focus On Sports, 4–5; Time Life Pictures/Hansel Mieth, 7
Les Banos, 21, 23
MLB photos via Getty Images Inc./Louis Requena, cover, 27; Photo File, 1, 15
National Baseball Hall of Fame, 25

Table of Contents

Chapter 1

Game Seven

Roberto Clemente was up. There were two outs in the top of the fourth inning. It was the final game of the 1971 World Series. The Pittsburgh Pirates and the Baltimore Orioles were locked in a scoreless tie.

Clemente's team had struggled against the Orioles pitcher. Eleven Pittsburgh batters had come to the plate. None had reached base.

The pitcher snapped a curveball toward Clemente. It hung high and outside. Clemente swung. His bat smacked the ball toward the fence. Two Orioles outfielders chased the ball, but it sailed into the stands.

Roberto Clemente had 12 hits in the 1971 World Series.

Clemente's team hung on to the lead. The Pirates were champions.

Afterward, Clemente was interviewed for TV. He spoke to his parents and others watching TV back in Puerto Rico. He told them it was the proudest day of his life.

Chapter 2

Puerto Rican Boyhood

Roberto Clemente was born August 18, 1934, in Carolina, Puerto Rico. He was the youngest child of Melchor and Luisa Walker Clemente. The family included seven other children.

Melchor worked as a foreman at a nearby sugar plantation. Roberto's mother washed other people's clothes for money. She made extra money by making lunches for sugar workers. The couple earned enough to feed and clothe everyone in the family. However, the family had no money for extras such as toys and sporting goods.

Puerto Rican farmhands like Clemente's father worked to cut and gather the tall sugar cane plants.

Working Hard

As a young boy, Clemente saw a used bicycle for sale. He told his father he wanted it. His father said Roberto would have to pay for it.

Roberto earned money delivering milk. He was paid one penny a day. He also did odd jobs to earn extra money. In three years, he saved enough to buy himself a used bicycle.

Learning the Game

When Roberto Clemente was young, his older siblings taught him how to play softball. Clemente fell in love with the game.

QUOTE

"I started playing baseball in the neighborhood before I was old enough to go to school . . . We played until it got so dark we couldn't see."

—Roberto Clemente

At age 5, Clemente often carried a rubber ball. He would bounce it off a wall and catch it. He practiced anywhere he could, even inside his bedroom.

Clemente and his friends played ball on a nearby field. The muddy ground was full of trees and weeds. The kids did not mind. They played for hours and hours. Clemente later remembered one game that stretched for more than eight hours. He said he smacked 10 home runs that day.

When Clemente (back row, center) got older, he began playing for organized teams.

Chapter 3

A Young Star

Clemente became a star **athlete** at Vizcarrondo High School in Carolina. He was a member of the track team, but Clemente really shined on the baseball field. He wasn't a big kid, but he swung the bat with surprising power. And he showed speed on the bases.

At age 18, Clemente tried out for the Santurce Crabbers. The Crabbers were part of the Puerto Rican Winter League. Clemente was young and had only a torn glove to play with. Still, the Crabbers liked what they saw. They gave him a **contract** and a new glove.

Clemente played for the Santurce Crabbers in Puerto Rico.

In the winter league, Clemente played alongside pros. At the time, many Major League Baseball players went to Puerto Rico to play ball in winter. Clemente was still finishing high school. It was not easy to compete with the pros for playing time.

Big-League Prospect

Early in 1953, Clemente's strong play for the Crabbers caught the eye of several big-league teams. Clemente chose the Brooklyn Dodgers. He signed with the team for $10,000 soon after graduating from high school.

Clemente never played for the Dodgers. He was sent to the Dodgers' minor league squad in Montreal, Canada. He spent much of the season on the bench.

That year, Clemente was in a car accident. Back home in Puerto Rico, a drunk driver hit Clemente's car. Clemente injured his back. Back pains nagged him for the rest of his career.

FACT!

Clemente chose the number 21 for his uniform number because there are 21 letters in his full name, Roberto Clemente Walker.

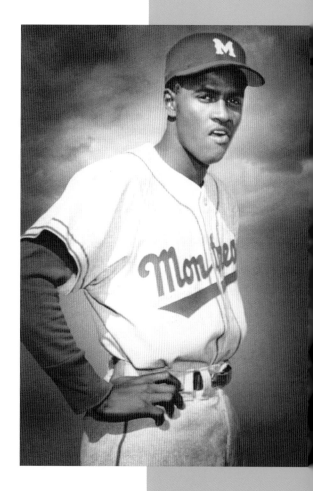

Clemente spent the 1954 season with the Brooklyn Dodgers' minor league team in Montreal, Canada. ➡

Chapter 4

To the Majors

In 1955, Clemente joined the Pittsburgh Pirates. At the time, the Pirates were at the bottom of the National League. Clemente was a **rookie** right fielder. He had a strong arm and fast feet. At the plate and on the bases, he showed flashes of greatness. He even smacked 11 triples. But his batting average was .255, well below what he hoped for.

Overcoming Barriers

Clemente found challenges on and off the field. Clemente had to learn a new language and a new way of life in the United States. He faced **discrimination** like he had never experienced.

Clemente had a strong throwing arm. In five seasons, he led the National League in throwing out base runners.

"If I am good enough to play, I have to be good enough to be treated like the rest of the players."
—Roberto Clemente

Latinos had played in the Major Leagues as far back as 1871. But the number of Latino players had been small. Baseball began to change when Jackie Robinson, an African American, joined the league. The sport was more open to players of color.

Like African American players, Latino players faced discrimination. Clemente and other Latinos were not welcome at restaurants that served whites only. At spring training in Florida, Clemente was not allowed to stay at the hotel with his white teammates.

A Championship Year

The 1960 season was Clemente's best yet at the plate. His team won the National League pennant. The Pirates met the mighty New York Yankees in the World Series. The Yankees were expected to win easily. But the Pirates pulled off an upset. Pittsburgh won the championship for the first time since 1925.

Clemente (front row, third from left) was one of few colored players on the 1960 Pirates team. ⬇

Chapter 5

All-Star Seasons

Clemente's greatest success began in the 1961 season. That year, he batted .351. Of his 201 hits, 23 were homers. He also won the National League batting title and was an All-Star. And he won his first Golden Glove award for his skill in right field.

Family Life

Between seasons, Clemente always returned home to Puerto Rico. There, he met Vera Zabala in January 1964.

The two were married in November of that year. A crowd of 1,500 went to the wedding in his hometown of Carolina. Thousands more filled a city plaza to celebrate.

Clemente married Vera Zabala in November 1964.

Clemente was an All-Star 12 times. He was named the National League's most valuable player, or MVP, in 1966. In 1967, he batted a career high.

Clemente and the Pirates reached the World Series again in 1971. Clemente's homer put the Pirates ahead for good in the final game. He was named the MVP of the World Series.

Chasing 3,000

Clemente began the 1972 season 118 hits short of 3,000 for his career. Only 10 players before him had reached that mark.

Entering the final weekend of the season, Clemente was stuck on 2,999. But a double against the New York Mets made him the first Latino to get 3,000 hits.

As Pittsburgh fans cheered, Clemente tipped his cap. It turned out that hit would be his last.

Clemente smacked the ball to the outfield for his 3,000th hit. ▼

Chapter 6

A Sudden End

After the 1972 season, Clemente returned home to his family in Puerto Rico. He and his wife had three sons. The oldest was 6 years old.

Nicaraguan Earthquake

In December 1972, an earthquake hit the Central American nation of Nicaragua. Thousands of people died. Many more were left homeless.

Clemente decided to help. He led an effort to collect donations for the people of Nicaragua.

On December 31, 1972, Clemente boarded a plane loaded with food and supplies. The flight took off from San Juan, Puerto Rico, at 9:20 at night.

Clemente posed with his wife and three sons before a game.

The plane was overloaded. Within minutes, the engines failed. The plane exploded in a ball of flames and crashed into the Atlantic Ocean. Just three months after getting his 3,000th hit, Clemente died.

▲ Clemente enjoyed signing autographs for children.

Helping Others

For years, Clemente had wished to help Puerto Rican children. He had raised funds for a place for children to learn about sports. After the plane crash, Clemente's wife led an effort to build the Roberto Clemente Sports City. Today Puerto Rico's children can go there to learn and enjoy baseball, softball, basketball, swimming, and many other sports.

In 1973, Roberto Clemente was voted into the National Baseball Hall of Fame in Cooperstown, New York. Usually, players cannot get into the Hall of Fame until five years after they quit playing. The Hall of Fame dropped that rule for Clemente. He was the first Latin-born ballplayer voted into the Hall of Fame.

The National Baseball Hall of Fame honored Clemente in 1973.

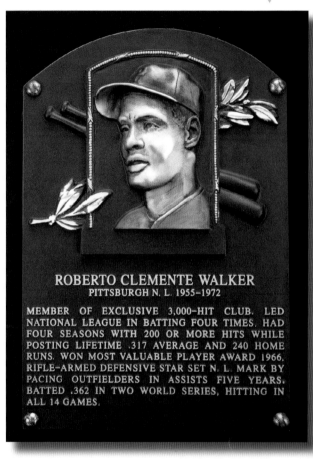

ROBERTO CLEMENTE WALKER
PITTSBURGH N. L. 1955–1972

MEMBER OF EXCLUSIVE 3,000-HIT CLUB. LED NATIONAL LEAGUE IN BATTING FOUR TIMES. HAD FOUR SEASONS WITH 200 OR MORE HITS WHILE POSTING LIFETIME .317 AVERAGE AND 240 HOME RUNS. WON MOST VALUABLE PLAYER AWARD 1966. RIFLE-ARMED DEFENSIVE STAR SET N. L. MARK BY PACING OUTFIELDERS IN ASSISTS FIVE YEARS. BATTED .362 IN TWO WORLD SERIES, HITTING IN ALL 14 GAMES.

FACT!

The Pittsburgh Pirates retired Clemente's number 21 in 1973. That means no other Pirate will wear that number.

Clemente's son stands in front of the large statue honoring Clemente at PNC Park in Pittsburgh.

Lasting Legacy

Clemente's death was a tragedy for his family, for Puerto Rico, and for baseball fans. He will always be remembered for his great playing. Today, he is also recalled for his good deeds. Each year, Major League Baseball gives out the Roberto Clemente Award. The award goes to the player who does the most to help others in his community.

Fast Facts

Full name: Roberto Clemente Walker

Birth: August 18, 1934

Death: December 31, 1972

Parents: Melchor Clemente and Luisa Walker Clemente

Siblings: Three brothers, one sister, two half brothers, one half sister

Wife: Vera Zabala

Sons: Roberto Jr., Enrique, Luis

Education: Vizcarrondo High School

Career hits: 3,000

Career games: 2,433

Career home runs: 240

Career RBIs: 1,305

Career batting average: .317

Golden Glove awards: 12

All-Star games: 12

National League MVP: 1966

World Series MVP: 1971

Time Line

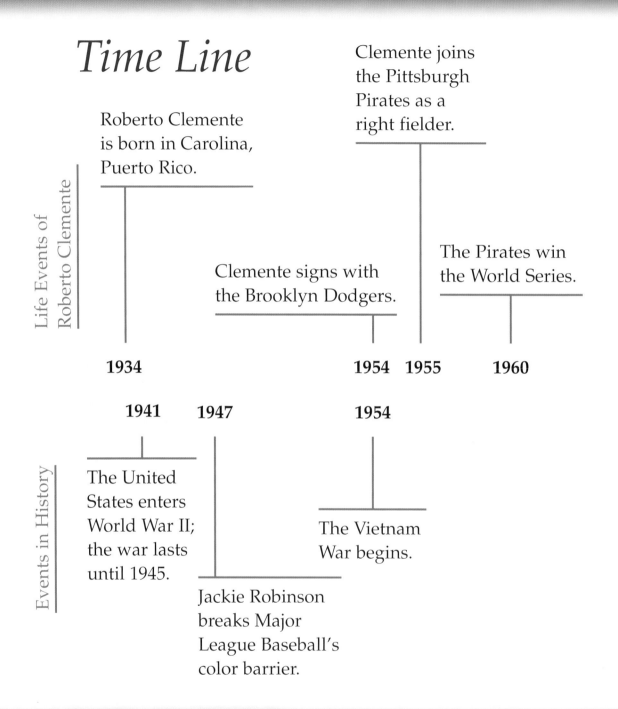

Life Events of Roberto Clemente

Roberto Clemente is born in Carolina, Puerto Rico.

1934

Clemente signs with the Brooklyn Dodgers.

Clemente joins the Pittsburgh Pirates as a right fielder.

1954

The Pirates win the World Series.

1955

1960

1941

1947

1954

Events in History

The United States enters World War II; the war lasts until 1945.

Jackie Robinson breaks Major League Baseball's color barrier.

The Vietnam War begins.

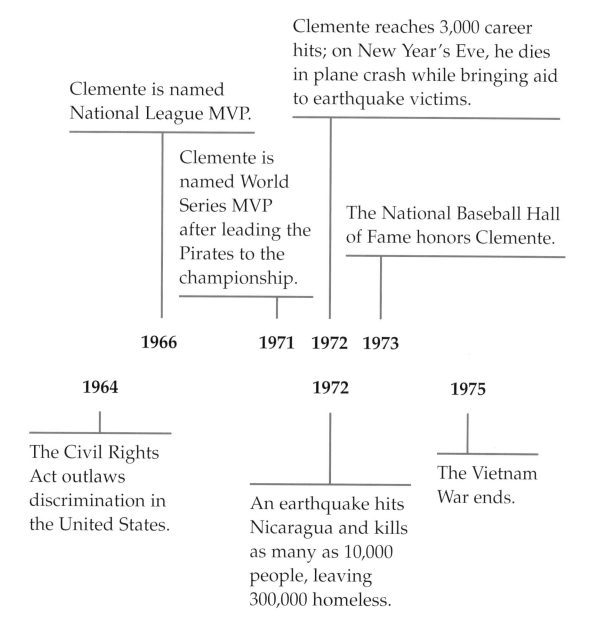

Clemente is named National League MVP.

Clemente reaches 3,000 career hits; on New Year's Eve, he dies in plane crash while bringing aid to earthquake victims.

Clemente is named World Series MVP after leading the Pirates to the championship.

The National Baseball Hall of Fame honors Clemente.

1966

1971 1972 1973

1964

1972

1975

The Civil Rights Act outlaws discrimination in the United States.

An earthquake hits Nicaragua and kills as many as 10,000 people, leaving 300,000 homeless.

The Vietnam War ends.

Glossary

athlete (ATH-lete)—someone who is trained in or skilled at a sport or game

contract (KON-trakt)—a legal agreement between a team and a player; contracts determine players' salaries.

discrimination (diss-krim-i-NAY-shuhn)—prejudice or unjust behavior to others based on differences in age, race, gender, or other traits

Latino (lah-TEE-noh)—a person who was born in or lives in Latin America

rookie (RUK-ee)—an athlete who is in his or her first season with a major league pro sports team

Internet Sites

FactHound offers a safe, fun way to find Internet sites related to this book. All of the sites on FactHound have been researched by our staff.

Here's how:

1. Visit *www.facthound.com*
2. Type in this special code **0736854428** for age-appropriate sites. Or enter a search word related to this book for a more general search.
3. Click on the **Fetch It** button.

FactHound will fetch the best sites for you!

Read More

Fischer, David. *Roberto Clemente.* Trailblazers of the Modern World. Milwaukee: World Almanac Library, 2005.

Silverstone, Michael. *Latino Legends: Hispanics in Major League Baseball.* High Five Reading. Bloomington, Minn.: Red Brick Learning, 2004.

Winter, Jonah. *Roberto Clemente: Pride of the Pittsburgh Pirates.* New York: Atheneum Books for Young Readers, 2005.

Index